Tw Upon a Time

John Dougherty

Illustrated by Emi Ordás

Contents

OXFORD
UNIVERSITY PRESS

Once Upon a Time

Chapter 1

Once upon a time – the time being about a quarter to nine last Tuesday morning – a boy named Will left his house to go to school.

Will was good-hearted, but bad at noticing things. So he didn't notice that one of the frogs croaking by the pond at number 33 had a small golden crown on its head.

Nor did he notice that Samson, the ginger cat from number 14, was wearing a very fetching pair of black shiny boots with long pink laces.

A lot of people leave their houses in a hurry at that time of the morning, and on this particular morning there were two such people leaving the house by the corner shop. One was a wolf wearing a lacy nightie and the other was an angry-looking man wearing a lumberjack shirt and waving an axe. Both were running, but the wolf was running slightly faster. Will did not notice either of them.

He did, however, notice the three strange old women by the crossing. It would have been difficult not to, since they were blocking the pavement in front of him.

'Your pardon, young sir,' said the first strange old woman. 'Might we beg your assistance in traversing this great highway?'

'Er ... ' Will said, not really understanding.

'Aye,' croaked the second, 'for it is so wide, and the vehicles upon it so strange and fast.'

This was no clearer. 'Er ... ' said Will again.

'What they mean,' said the third old woman, glancing impatiently at the others, 'is would you help us cross the road, please?'

The first two glared at her.

'Oh,' Will said, pressing the button. 'Oh. Er ... Yes. Of course.' The lights changed and he led the way across the road.

'You,' the first old woman hissed to the third, 'have no sense of tradition.'

'Tradition be blowed,' said the third. 'You've got to move with the times, Sibyl. There's no point in saying things people don't understand.'

'Here we are,' said Will, as they reached the other side.

'Our thanks, young sir,' said the first old woman. 'You are good, and kind, and noble of heart, and so we shall grant you three gifts.'

'Er ... my mum says I shouldn't accept things from strangers ... ' Will began, but the first old woman ignored this.

'You are fair of speech ... ' she said.

'He's not really,' the third old woman pointed out. 'He says "er" all the time.'

'*You are fair of speech*,' the first one insisted, glaring again at the third. 'So I give you this gift: when you speak, pearls shall fall from your lips.'

'Aye,' said the second, 'and you are fair of face, but from this day on you shall be fairer and more handsome still.'

The third thought for a moment. 'And you shall have chips for lunch every day, and never get fat or spotty. *What*?' she added, seeing the looks the other two were giving her. 'It's a good gift!'

'Since when were *chips* a fairy gift?' the first

one demanded grumpily, as she hobbled away. 'You've got *no* idea of the way things ought to be done, has she, Delphine?'

'Absolutely right,' agreed the second old woman. 'What's next? Testing for princesses by putting a *chip* underneath twenty mattresses? Magic chips that grow into a giant *chip*stalk?'

'You two have no idea about modern kids,' the third one grumbled. 'And why are you both hobbling? There's nothing wrong with your legs!'

'It's tradition!' the first two chorused irritably.

The third old woman strode angrily down the road, with the other two hobbling after her.

Will waved uncertainly as he watched them go.

Chapter 2

The first bell was ringing as Will ran into the playground. Mrs Squiggins, the head teacher, was ringing it. She was a huge and fearsome woman with a long nose, a short temper and more than the usual number of chins. When she got cross, which was often, most of the chins wobbled furiously like angry, upside down jellies.

'Almost late, William,' she growled, looming over him like a vast and threatening thundercloud. Then she bent down, her face drawing closer to his until he could see two small hairs sticking up like evil little bunny ears from the large mole on her cheek.

'Are you wearing make-up?' she demanded loudly.

Fraser Gribblethwaite, slipping into the line in front of Will, sniggered unpleasantly.

Will stared. What on earth would make her think that? Embarrassed beyond words, he shook his head firmly.

Mrs Squiggins squinted at him. 'There's something different about you,' she said suspiciously. 'Are you sure you're not wearing make-up?' She licked one fleshy thumb, wiped it across his left eyelid and examined it carefully.

All eyes were on them now. In front of Fraser, Seema Roy giggled. 'Will's wearing make-up!' she whispered to Tasha Okewundo.

Will's face grew hotter. 'I'm not!' he protested.

Something fell from his mouth and landed with a *clack!* on the hard surface of the playground. Mrs Squiggins looked down, chins vibrating menacingly.

'Sweets? In school?'

'I ... ' Will began. There was another *clack!*

The chins were rippling now, like waves on the sea as a storm rises.

'Any more in there?'

Will shook his head, checking with his tongue to make sure.

Mrs Squiggins grabbed his face in one meaty hand. 'Let me see,' she ordered.

Will opened his mouth wide and Mrs Squiggins peered inside. 'Hmmm ... ' she said, sounding as though she half-suspected some of his teeth might be sweets in disguise. Then she pointed at the things on the ground.

Will picked them up. They were hard and round and white and shiny. He could see why

Mrs Squiggins had thought they were sweets, but although they were wet from his mouth, they were not sticky. Not sweets, then. More like beads, or ...

He remembered the dotty old women at the crossing. Hadn't one of them said something about pearls dropping from his lips? She couldn't have meant *real* pearls, surely? *Actually* dropping from his lips? Yet ... here they were. Puzzled, he wiped them on his sleeve and went to put them in his pocket.

'William! That is *disgusting*!'

He looked up. Mrs Squiggins was staring at him, aghast as a duchess who has just watched one of the footmen blow his nose on the best tablecloth. Suddenly Will realized what she thought. She thought he had picked up two dirty sweets off the ground and put them in his pocket *to eat later*.

Blushing with embarrassment, he whipped the pearls from his pocket. 'Sorry, Miss!'

Too late, he felt another pearl drop from his lips.

Clack!

'Is that another sweet?' Mrs Squiggins' tone suggested that 'yes' was not a safe answer.

Panicked, Will fell to his knees and scooped it up. 'No! I just dropped one of the first two!'

Clack!

'Er ... that was the other one!' He snatched it up.

Clack!

'Oops! There goes the first one again!'

Clack!

'Er ... '

Clack!

'WILLIAM JACKSON!'

Will froze.

The entire playground froze.

The whole world froze.

Mrs Squiggins took in a long, angry breath through her long, angry nose, nostrils flaring like the mouths of two enraged monsters. Her pale, thin lips turned fiercely downwards, her chins wobbled as if the earth itself was quaking, but all she said – very, very quietly – was: 'Don't. Say. Another. Word. Just ... put them in the bin. Join the line. And go to class.'

Will nodded mutely. His legs shaking, he dropped two of the pearls into the bin with a loud metallic *clang!* and then he returned to the lined-up class, furtively slipping the remaining pearls into his trouser pocket.

Chapter 3

Will was hanging up his coat when he felt the sharp jab of a knuckle against his spine and a voice hissed, 'Give us a sweet then, little girly!'

Will turned. Fraser Gribblethwaite was grinning slyly at him, gleeful as a ferret who has cornered a nice plump rabbit. 'Go on,' he said spitefully. 'Give us a sweet. And not one that's been on the ground. We're not all mubblers.'

'Mubbler' was Fraser Gribblethwaite's favourite word. Nobody knew what it meant – probably not even Fraser Gribblethwaite – but somehow, when he used it, it sounded like the worst thing anybody could call you. Will felt himself redden.

Fraser's sly grin widened. 'Give us a sweet, little girly *mubbler*.' He poked Will hard in the ribs. Will stepped back and found himself pressed against the coat pegs.

'Leave him alone, Fraser,' said a firm voice.

Fraser rolled his eyes scornfully. 'What are you going to do, Seema? Think I'm scared of a *gir* … '

His voice died away as he turned to see not just Seema, but every girl in the class staring coldly at him and blockading the cloakroom exit.

'What's the matter, Fraser?' Seema asked. 'Not scared of a bunch of *girls*, are you?'

The group stepped forward. There was something unexpectedly menacing about them.

Unnerved, Fraser stepped back, and stood on Will's toe.

'Ow!' yelped Will. A pearl rolled out of his mouth and into the hood of Fraser's coat.

Seema's eyes narrowed dangerously and she glared at Fraser. 'Did you hurt him? You'd better not have hurt him!'

Fraser flinched. It was like seeing the ferret suddenly being terrorized by a baby guinea-pig. Then, recovering some of his bravado, he said, 'Oh, I get it. All the girls sticking up for another *girl*, right?'

'I'm *not* a girl!' Will said angrily, dribbling another pearl into Fraser's hood.

'Yeah,' said Seema, jabbing Fraser in the ribs. 'He's not a girl, so don't call him that, OK?'

'Not that there's anything wrong with being a girl,' added Courtney Glover firmly. 'So don't talk like there is, Fraser.'

Courtney was tall and athletic, and afraid of nothing. She could kick a football harder and straighter than anyone in the class, and – although none of them would have said so – she made most of the boys slightly nervous. If Fraser had any sense, he probably would have been nervous too; but if Fraser was short of anything, it was sense.

'Well, if he's not a *girl*, why's he wearing make-up, then?'

'I am *not* wearing make-up!' Will said furiously. All eyes were on Fraser, so none of the girls noticed a third pearl joining the others in Fraser's hood.

'Yeah, Fraser, he's *not* wearing make-up!' said Seema.

'Well, *you* said he was!' Fraser retorted. 'You said it to Tasha! I heard you!'

'Well, he's not, all right!' Seema snapped. 'He's just ... he's just naturally good-looking, OK?'

And to Will's horror, she blushed.

Worse still, some of the other girls blushed, too, and some of them giggled.

And even worse than that, Courtney Glover muttered, 'I think he *is* wearing make-up, actually.'

Will closed his eyes in despair. It was bad

enough dribbling pearls – which, he queasily remembered, were actually hard, shiny balls of oyster-spit – every time he spoke. Worse than that was the thought that every girl in the class might suddenly be in love with him. And worse than *that* was the thought that every girl in the class *except* Courtney Glover might suddenly be in love with him.

Not that he actually *wanted* her to be in love with him, of course; but if he had to have any girl in the class fall in love with him, it would be Courtney. Not only was she quite pretty, but she was probably more than a match for Fraser Gribblethwaite. He opened his eyes again and just at that moment, Mr Barker appeared.

'All right, what's the hold-up ... Oh. Fraser. I might have known you'd be at the centre of things.'

He didn't sound cross. In fact, the terrible thing about Mr Barker was that he was never cross. It was much, much worse than that.

He was *understanding*.

Even when someone had been really, really bad, instead of getting cross, Mr Barker would be *understanding* with them. He would go all soft-voiced and sympathetic, and ... *disappointed*. That was the worst thing, really. Mr Barker didn't even shout. He just ... *understood*.

More than once, Will had seen him *understanding* someone until they broke down in tears. There was a rumour that Mr Barker had once caught a gang of burglars breaking into his house and had just shaken his head, looked disappointed, then spent the rest of the night *understanding* them. Apparently, when Mr Barker had finished *understanding* them, the burglars had all gone to the nearest police station and handed themselves in, and when they came out of prison they went about feeding the poor and doing good.

The only person Mr Barker seemed unable to understand into sainthood was Fraser

Gribblethwaite. But then, nothing seemed to work on Fraser Gribblethwaite, who was now looking extremely indignant. 'What? I never done nothing!'

Mr Barker knew that when Fraser Gribblethwaite told you that he 'never done nothing', he had almost certainly been doing something; and he had almost certainly been doing it to somebody else; and the somebody else had almost certainly not been enjoying it.

'Are you all right, Will?' Mr Barker asked, his voice concerned.

Will nodded. 'Fine, sir,' he said into Fraser Gribblethwaite's hood.

Mr Barker looked around. 'Right, girls. Into class, please.'

The girls reluctantly left the cloakroom, most of them glancing longingly back at Will and one or two of them doing an odd little wave with their fingers.

'And you, Fraser.'

'But I never *done* nothing!'

'I'm sure you didn't, Fraser, but go to class, please. Now, Will, are you sure you're all right?'

Will nodded as sincerely as he could.

Mr Barker gave him a sympathetic look. 'Will,' he said understandingly, 'are you wearing make-up?'

Chapter 4

The morning went on being terrible.

Almost all of the girls wanted to sit next to Will because they thought he looked really lovely.

Almost none of the boys wanted to sit next to Will because they thought he was wearing make-up.

And absolutely nobody wanted to sit next to Fraser Gribblethwaite, because he was Fraser Gribblethwaite.

As a result, when Will came in and sat down with some of the other boys, they got up and moved to another table. Straight away, every girl in the class – apart from Courtney Glover – tried to sit in the chair next to his.

Mr Barker took over and within moments Will found himself sitting at a circular table with Courtney Glover, Fraser Gribblethwaite, Jamie Carson and Seema Roy.

Happiest with this arrangement was Seema, who was opposite Will. This meant that she could spend the morning smiling at him and trying to catch his eye. Least happy was Jamie, who was sitting right next to Will and kept edging away nervously, as if he was worried that wearing make-up was catching.

As for the other two, Courtney didn't seem bothered either way and Fraser Gribblethwaite, on Will's other side, kept pinching him and whispering, 'Give us a sweet, mubbler!'

It was hard for Will to keep focused on his

work. He had several things on his mind. Firstly: how was he going to manage if pearls kept falling out of his mouth? He tried to remember exactly what the first old woman had said. Was it just for today? What if it was for *ever*?

Secondly: why did everyone think he was wearing make-up? And why were all the girls – except for Courtney – being so soppy about him?

Thirdly: how could he get Fraser Gribblethwaite to stop pinching him and calling him a 'mubbler' and asking for sweets?

And fourthly: what on earth was this work about? What with all the thinking and worrying about the pearls and the make-up and Fraser Gribblethwaite, he'd sort of missed the bit where Mr Barker had told them what to do. He craned his neck sideways and tried to sneak a look at what Jamie was writing.

Jamie edged away nervously.

A sharp pinch at his side almost made Will

yell. He clapped his hand to his mouth in case another pearl popped out.

'Give us a sweet, you mubbler,' Fraser hissed.

His hand still in front of his face, Will whispered, 'I haven't got any. Stop pinching me.' He felt the small round hardness of another pearl, and then another, slip into his palm.

'You have,' insisted Fraser. 'I saw them in the playground. Give us one.'

'I haven't. I wouldn't give you one if I did, though. Ow!' The 'Ow!' was because Fraser had pinched him again.

Three more pearls trickled into Will's hand. Carefully, and covering his mouth with the other hand, Will transferred them into his pocket. 'I said, stop pinching me!'

'Leave him alone, Fraser,' said Courtney, without looking up from her work.

Fraser scowled, pinched Will once more for luck and then left him alone. For a few minutes, anyway.

Chapter 5

Break time was no better. The other boys grudgingly allowed Will to join in a kickabout – or, at least, they didn't stop him from joining in, but nobody actually passed to him, or let him get close enough to tackle them, so it was fairly boring. Besides, the game was a bit spoiled by all the girls who kept 'accidentally' wandering across the pitch and stopping to chat to Will.

In the end, he went and hid in the toilets. And there, of course, he looked in the mirror above the basin, and his eyes widened at what he saw.

He didn't look the same.

It was clearly him, but his eyes were brighter, his lips redder and fuller, his eyelashes longer and darker. His skin glowed with health, his hair was glossy; even his eyebrows seemed more shapely. He looked like a film star.

Of course people thought he was wearing make-up. He wondered if his mum had played a trick on him. Perhaps she had crept into his room with her make-up kit while he was asleep and painted his face?

But then ... hadn't the second old woman by the crossing said something about him being more handsome? And ... wasn't there something a bit weird about the walk to school this morning? Vague memories of things he'd seen but hadn't noticed began to prickle at the back of his mind.

Well, he thought, *let's look at it rationally.* Which was more likely – that some dotty old women straight out of a fairy tale had performed magic on him, or that his mum had played a silly trick?

Put like that, it was obvious. It *had* to be magic. There was no way his mum would ever do anything so daft; she was the most sensible person he knew. Anyway, there were the pearls to consider.

That was when it occurred to him that maybe if he kept speaking, he'd eventually run out of pearls. Will spent the rest of break time locked in a cubicle, mumbling. He discovered fairly quickly that you can't flush pearls away and he returned to class at the end of break with his pockets bulging and no sign of the pearls running out.

And then things got even worse.

Chapter 6

As Will entered the classroom, Fraser
Gribblethwaite grabbed him and sat on his
head. Will kicked and struggled, but Fraser
Gribblethwaite held him down until the
classroom door opened and Mr Barker said,
'Fraser!'

You could tell from Mr Barker's voice that
he was very disappointed with Fraser.

You could tell from the slow and deliberate way that Fraser stood up, pushing down hard on Will's head, that Fraser didn't care.

Mr Barker turned to Will, his voice filled with understanding. 'Are you all right?'

Having his head trapped underneath Fraser Gribblethwaite had not been a pleasant experience for Will – for a number of reasons – and he was a little disorientated. 'Er ... yeah,' he said dazedly.

The room went quiet as something small and white fell from Will's mouth and landed with a *clack!* on the floor.

Mr Barker's eyes widened. 'Will,' he said quietly, 'I think you've lost a tooth.'

Several of the girls screamed and Seema Roy fainted – or at least pretended to faint – the way she'd seen someone do in a film once, but nobody was convinced so after a moment she got up again.

Quickly, Will scooped the pearl up.

'Are you OK?' Mr Barker continued. Will nodded. 'You'd better run along to the bathroom and rinse your mouth.'

Will left hurriedly, leaving Fraser Gribblethwaite to face the full, untamed force of Mr Barker's disappointment, and stayed in the toilets just long enough to be convincing.

All was quiet by the time he returned and Fraser Gribblethwaite had been made to change places with Courtney, which meant at least he couldn't pinch Will – although he did manage to pass him a note across the table. The note read:

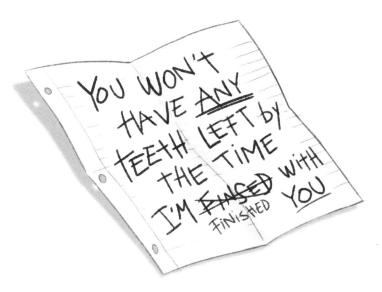

Chapter 7

As soon as Mr Barker dismissed them, Will
was out of the door. Fraser Gribblethwaite was
clearly furious. He seemed to believe it was
Will's fault that Mr Barker thought he'd
knocked Will's tooth out.

So Will ran. The pearls in his overfull pockets
dug painfully into his thighs, but he ignored the
discomfort. If he could only get to the dining
hall, he would be safe.

Through the school he raced, dodging and weaving to avoid knocking over the smaller children. Fraser Gribblethwaite had no such qualms. Behind him, Will could hear the sounds of little people hitting the floor. His heart pounded, but hope rose within him; he was almost there …

'WILLIAM JACKSON!'

The dread sound of Mrs Squiggins' voice, rich with outrage, brought him to a halt. He turned, trembling. The infuriated head teacher was marching towards him, her face blazing red and her nose pointing at him like a nuclear missile.

'What *has* got into you?' she bellowed. 'We do *not* run in the corridors!'

Will's hand went to his mouth. 'Sorry, Miss! Sorry!' he blurted. He scooped the unseen pearls from his lips and pushed them desperately into his bulging pocket.

Then, two things happened at once. As Mrs Squiggins reached the corner, Fraser Gribblethwaite shot out from the other corridor and collided with her; and the lining of Will's pocket tore. An avalanche of pearls tumbled down his trouser leg and spilled onto the floor beneath their feet.

Suddenly, Mrs Squiggins and Fraser Gribblethwaite were rolling and skittering uncontrollably along the corridor; legs flailing, arms windmilling frantically and eyes wide with panic as the pearls spun like crazy little wheels beneath them.

'Woooooooooooooaaaaaahhhhhhh!' cried Fraser Gribblethwaite.

'Waaaaaaaaaauuuuuugggghhhhhh!' yelled Mrs Squiggins.

Will leapt out of the way just in time.

With a piteous wail, Fraser Gribblethwaite tottered, tipped, toppled and tumbled. His legs shot out from beneath him. For a single moment he was airborne and then with a mighty crash he flopped to the floor.

And Mrs Squiggins fell on top of him.

Once more, the whole world seemed to freeze. Mrs Squiggins rose like a monster from the deep. Towering over them, a vast volcano about to erupt, she gazed down upon the scene and knew beyond doubt who was to blame.

'Fraser Gribblethwaite!' she roared, lifting Fraser by the collar. 'Chasing other children in the corridors! Bashing into me! Scattering these beads all over the floor! Come with me at once!'

Still ranting, she dragged him down the corridor to her office.

And Will, with a tremendous sense of relief, went in to lunch.

Chapter 8

It was Tuesday. That meant soggy potatoes. Will reluctantly held out his plate. A huge scoop of chips – crisp, golden, perfect chips – was ladled onto it. He looked up.

The three dinner ladies at the counter weren't the usual ones, but Will recognized them. His jaw dropped.

'Well, young sir,' said the first. 'Have our gifts been to your liking and a cause of great pleasure to your noble self?'

'Er ... ' said Will.

'Aye,' croaked the second, 'and have the fair young maidens, one and all, been struck by your great beauty?'

'Er ... ' said Will again. 'Er ... '

'Oh, for goodness' sake, stop it, you two,' said the third. 'He's dribbling pearls into his dinner.' She turned to Will. 'Has it been OK so far?'

'Er ... ' said Will, 'not really.'

The first two old women looked startled. 'What?' said the first. 'Have the fairy gifts not set you on the path to fortune?'

'Er ... well, no,' said Will. The third old woman held a bowl in front of his mouth. 'They set me on the path to having Fraser Gribblethwaite sit on my head.'

'Tell us, child,' croaked the second. 'What has come to pass?'

'Er ... ' said Will.

'She means,' sighed the third old woman, 'tell us what's been happening.'

Will told them.

'Stop,' said the first, after some time. 'I see our gifts have led to misfortune. Moreover, the bowl overfloweth and I have pearls down the front of my blouse.'

'Told you,' said the third. The first two ignored her.

'So,' said the first, 'no more shall pearls fall from your lips.'

'Thank you,' said Will. Then he said, 'Er ... hello! Um ... three blind mice! Peter Piper picked a peck of pickled pepper! I'm a banana, la la la!'

No pearls fell. Will breathed a sigh of relief. 'Thank you,' he said again; and meant it.

'But *my* gift surely you wish to keep?' croaked the second old woman.

'Er ... ' said Will. 'Well ... I don't want to seem

ungrateful, but I'd rather people liked me for who I really am. The attention my face has got today … '

The old woman sighed. 'Be as you were before,' she said.

'How are the chips?' asked the third.

Will tried one. 'They're perfect!' he said. 'The best chips I've ever tasted!' The old woman beamed. 'But … er … ' Will hesitated.

'Go on,' said the old woman encouragingly.

'Well … ' said Will. 'I just … if I had them every day, I just wonder if I might stop appreciating them.'

The old woman smiled. 'How about if I grant you the *option* of chips every day?'

Will grinned. 'That'd be great! Thanks!'

He set his tray on a nearby table, then turned to smile at the old ladies again.

They weren't there. The usual dinner ladies stood in their place.

Will shrugged, smiled to himself and began to eat.

Suddenly, a shadow fell across his plate. He turned round.

'Hi, Will!' said Seema. Then the huge smile on her face vanished. 'Oh,' she added.

'Oh,' echoed most of the other girls standing behind her.

As one, they moved off.

'He's not really that good-looking after all, is he?' he heard one of them say.

'Maybe he *was* wearing make-up,' another muttered.

Only one remained behind.

'You've been acting really oddly today,' said Courtney Glover, sitting down opposite him. 'Talking with your hand over your mouth, wearing make-up ... I'm curious. What's going on?'

'Well,' said Will, 'if you must know, I met three old women who gave me fairy gifts. One said that pearls would drop from my lips when I spoke, one said I'd be really handsome, and one said I'd have chips for lunch every day.'

Courtney gave him a sceptical look. 'Do you think I'm daft?' she said. 'Chips every day? Who's going to believe that?'

Once More Upon a Time

Chapter 1

Courtney Glover was on her way to school one day when she met a wolf.

'Hello, pretty little girl,' said the wolf. 'And where might you be off to on this fine morning?'

Courtney looked warily at the wolf. 'I'm not supposed to talk to strangers,' she said. 'Anyway, you're a wolf; and sorry, but that's just weird.'

The wolf had a feeling that this was not how the conversation was meant to go. 'I suppose you're going to visit your poorly old grandma,' it suggested, 'and you're taking some goodies to her?'

'That's not goodies,' said Courtney. 'That's my book bag. Now, would you get out of my way, please?'

The wolf scratched its head. It was not a particularly clever wolf, but it knew what was supposed to happen, and it couldn't understand why it wasn't happening now. It decided to go back to the beginning and start again.

'Hello, pretty little girl,' it said. 'And where might you be off to on this fine morning?'

Courtney gave the wolf a hard stare. 'You already said that,' she pointed out. 'And don't keep calling me "pretty little girl". It's sexist.'

'No, that's wrong,' said the wolf. 'You're not supposed to say any of that. You're supposed to tell me where you're going and it's supposed to be your poorly old grandma's house.'

'I'm not going to my grandma's house, though, am I?' Courtney said. 'I'm going to school. And if you don't get out of my way, the head teacher'll come looking for me.'

'Is she a poorly old head teacher?' asked the wolf hopefully. 'Are you taking her some goodies as she lies ill in bed?'

'No,' said Courtney. 'She's not even slightly ill. She's really, really healthy. And strong. And she hates wolves.'

'Look, shall we try again?' said the wolf. 'Maybe you could change your mind and go and see your poorly old grandma? After all,' it added disapprovingly, 'what sort of girl doesn't go and see her poorly old grandma, who's lying in bed all poorly and ... and poorly, and just waiting for some goodies to make her feel better before she gets gobbled up?

Answer me that!'

Courtney gave the wolf another hard stare. She was good at hard stares. In fact, Courtney's hard stares were about the only thing that worked against Fraser Gribblethwaite, the class bully.

However, the wolf was – somewhat surprisingly – even less intelligent than Fraser Gribblethwaite, and didn't seem to notice that it was being given a hard stare.

'Look,' said Courtney. 'I'm *not* going to see my poorly old grandma – and even if I *was*, I wouldn't tell you, because you're a wolf. So could you just get out of my way?'

The wolf stared at her, perplexed. Then it had an idea.

'Hello, pretty little girl,' it said. 'And where might you be off to on this fine morning?'

At this point, Courtney lost patience with the wolf and hit it with her book bag. Unfortunately for the wolf, Courtney was an avid reader, and that morning her bag contained a copy of *Harry Potter and the Order of the Phoenix*. In hardback.

The wolf groaned pitifully as Courtney stepped lightly over it and hurried on her way to school. It was a shame she'd had to use violence, she thought; it wasn't the wolf's fault it was so dim. She might even have felt a little bit sorry for it if it hadn't been so annoying. A bit like Fraser Gribblethwaite.

Chapter 2

As Courtney approached the crossing, she noticed three strange-looking old women huddled together, talking excitedly.

'Well, I have to say, I enjoyed that!' said one of them.

'Did you see the look on his face?' cackled the second.

'Before or after?' the first one snickered.

'I'm still not sure we should have done it,' said the third, slightly regretfully.

'He deserved it!' snapped the first one.

'Definitely,' said the second.

'Well – probably,' said the third. 'But ... we don't even know what "mubblers" means.'

'It was something bad,' said the first. 'You could tell by the way he said it.'

'Yes, but we shouldn't have lost our tempers like that,' insisted the third. 'Not all of us at the same time! Still, at least we all went for frog.'

'Frog?' said the first. 'I thought we were doing toad!'

'Ah,' said the second worriedly. 'Um ... I *thought* he looked a bit amphibious for a rat.'

The third groaned despairingly. 'This is bad,' she said. 'If I did frog, and you did toad, and Delphine did rat *at the same time* ... well, you know what that means.'

'Don't worry,' said the first old woman soothingly. 'It'll be all right in the end. It always is. We just need to wait for ... '

The second old woman cleared her throat and indicated Courtney, who was listening curiously.

'And there she is!' the first one said hopefully. She turned to Courtney and said, 'Your pardon, young lady. Might we beg your assistance in traversing this great highway?'

'Aye,' croaked the second, 'for it is so wide, and the vehicles upon it … '

'We don't have time for this!' the third one broke in. 'We've messed up and we need to sort it out! Listen, Courtney – it is Courtney, isn't it? – we know you're good and noble and kind and would help us out if we asked, so from this day on … '

'Hang on,' said Courtney quickly. Will – one of the boys in her class – had once told her a story about meeting three strange old women. She had always thought he'd made the whole thing up, but it was suddenly very clear that he hadn't. 'I don't mean to be rude, but you're not going to make pearls start dropping from my lips or anything, are you?'

'Not at all,' said the third old woman. 'That would be ridiculous, wouldn't it, Sibyl?' This was addressed meaningfully to the first, who blushed and looked at her feet. 'No, I give you this gift: that from this day on you will understand the speech of animals.'

'Particularly frogs and rats and toads,' put in the second old woman.

'*All* animals,' said the third old woman firmly.

'*Especially* frogs and rats and toads, though,' the first old woman said.

'Just let *me* do this, will you!' snapped the third. '*All* animals. Just in case. You will understand the speech of *all* animals.'

'Um ... I think maybe I can do that already, actually,' said Courtney. 'I was having a chat with a wolf just now.'

'Did it keep going on about your poorly old grandma?' the third old woman asked. 'That wolf will talk to anyone. No, this is a proper fairy gift and no mistake. Any questions?'

'Can I turn it on and off?'

'What?' said the third old woman. 'Oh, erm ... yes, I suppose so. Just tweak your earlobe.'

'All right, then,' Courtney said. 'Um ... thanks.'

'You're welcome,' said the third old woman. 'Have a nice day.'

The women turned to go. Courtney stood for a moment, listening to them.

'*Have a nice day* indeed,' the first one was grumbling. 'What sort of fairy blessing is that?'

'It's not a fairy blessing, Sibyl. It's just what people say!' the third protested.

'Well, I don't hold with it,' the first old woman muttered. 'What do you think, Delphine?'

'Me?' said the second. 'I think some people need a sense of tradition!'

'Oh, tradition be blowed! I keep telling you, you've got to move with the times!' said the third. 'And ... Hang on, you're hobbling again! Why are you hobbling? Hobbling's for people with sore legs!'

'We *like* hobbling,' Sibyl said sulkily. 'Hobbling's good for you.'

'Anyway,' added Delphine, 'I wonder you're not hobbling, Tracy. I'd have thought your feet would be *aching*, seeing as you're too big for your boots!'

And then the light changed, and Courtney hurried across the road.

Chapter 3

A little further along Courtney's route, a sweet little robin perched on a fence, chirping merrily. Courtney looked at her watch. School didn't start for another ten minutes; she had time to try out her new gift.

'Hello!' she said, tweaking her earlobe.

The little bird tipped its head cutely to one side, one bright eye fixed curiously on her. Then it opened its beak and yelled a rude word.

'Er ... pardon?' said Courtney.

'Go away!' shouted the bird – or rather, something that meant 'go away', but was much, much ruder. 'Clear off! This is my patch! Go on, get out of it, or I'll rip your head off! I'll chop you up with my bare beak! Clear *off*!'

There were more rude words, as well. Courtney, who – even though she was in the same class as Fraser Gribblethwaite – had never heard such terrible language before, blushed as red as the robin's chest. 'But ... ' she began.

'Fear me!' the little robin shrieked.

I am the **Destroyer**! Depart,
lest this moment be your last!
Clear off before I *tweet*!

Without thinking, Courtney had put her hand to her earlobe and tweaked. Instantly, the bird's ravings had turned back into melodious chirpings. Intrigued, she tweaked a few more times.

Tweet tweet tweeety tweet-tweet tweet warning you, buster, tweet, tweet last chance, tweet tweety tweeeet tweet out of my territory tweet-tweet tweettweettweet tweet, **IF YOU KNOW WHAT'S GOOD FOR YOU!**

Courtney walked on, listening carefully. In the park across the road, a dog was frolicking madly, exclaiming, 'Hey! Wow! Wow, brilliant! Amazing! Wow!' at everything, while another was chasing it, shouting, 'Play! Let's play!'

On the path in front of her, a small black cat looked up with haughty, unblinking eyes. Courtney bent down and stroked it behind the ears.

'Very good, slave,' the cat said lazily. 'A little more to the left.' Then it stiffened. 'Toy!' it said excitedly.

Courtney followed its gaze. It was staring at a frog – or perhaps a toad – which was sitting about a metre away. Suddenly the cat sprang, batting at the frog, which shrieked in alarm.

'Ow!' it yelled. 'Stop! Get off!'

'Ha!' said the cat. 'Try to get away from me, would you?'

'Help!' wailed the frog.

Quickly, Courtney picked it up. 'There you go,' she said. 'You want to be more careful, froggy.'

The frog glared at her. 'Shut up, *mubbler*,' it said.

Chapter 4

Courtney stared. Only one person in the world, as far as she knew, ever used the word 'mubbler', and he wasn't green and amphibious. Or, at least, he wasn't usually; but as she stared at the frog – or was it a toad? – she thought about what the old women had been saying ...

And suddenly it all made sense. Courtney looked at the small creature in her hand. 'Fraser?'

The frog scowled at her. 'What, *mubbler*?' it said.

That settled it.

'You've been turned into a frog, haven't you?' she said.

'No,' the frog said defensively. 'I never done nothing.'

'Were you rude to three old women?'

'Those old mubblers? What if I was? Leave me alone.'

'You mean, put you down?' Courtney said. 'On the pavement? Next to the cat?'

'Yes!' said the cat, circling Courtney's ankles impatiently. 'Give me my toy at once, slave!'

The frog said nothing, but looked sulky – a look which, it has to be said, comes fairly easily to a frog.

'Look,' said Courtney. 'You're in big trouble. You've been rude to three ... witches, or fairies, or something, and they've turned you into a frog. It sounds like they've messed up the spell, so anything might happen. You'd better stay with me till we work out what to do. And – oh, my gosh, we're going to be late!' She had suddenly noticed the time. Courtney popped Fraser into the pocket of her fleece and ran.

The bell was ringing as Courtney dashed into the playground. That may be why she did not notice the *whooomph*-ing sound, like a sudden inrush of air, that came from her pocket.

The mood in the classroom that morning was lighter, sunnier and generally less nervous than usual. It was unknown for Fraser Gribblethwaite to be absent, and yet, inexplicably, there he wasn't. A spirit of celebration began to take hold. Everyone settled down to work with an unaccustomed happiness.

Everyone, that is, except Courtney, who knew exactly where Fraser was and was extremely worried that she might accidentally squash him. She felt she could not cope with this crisis by herself; she had to share it with someone. Very soon, her chance came.

'Courtney,' Mr Barker said. 'Could you take this folder to Mrs Squiggins for me, please?'

Courtney took the folder. 'Can I take someone with me?'

'Who would you like to take?' he asked.

Every girl in the class sat up straight and folded her arms. None of the boys bothered, because girls didn't take boys on errands.

Except this time.

'Will,' Courtney said.

There was a shocked silence, followed by an 'OoooooOOOOOOOOooooooh!' from most of the class.

Will blushed and hesitated. Many of the girls thought he had a soft spot for Courtney and they teased him about it sometimes. If he went on this errand with her, it would double the teasing.

On the other hand, Will actually did have a soft spot for Courtney, and if he went on this errand he could spend a bit of time with her without any of the girls sneaking up behind him and going 'OooooooOOOOOOOOooooooh!' in his ear. So he went.

As soon as they were in the corridor, Courtney said, 'Can you keep a secret?'

Will nodded.

Courtney leaned in closer and whispered, 'I've got Fraser Gribblethwaite in my pocket.'

Chapter 5

'What do you mean, you've got Fraser Gribblethwaite in your pocket?' Will asked.

'I mean,' said Courtney, 'he's been turned into a frog. Look.'

She produced the frog from her pocket. It gazed at her balefully. 'About time,' it said. 'Your pocket stinks like a mubbler.'

'See?' Courtney said.

Will eyed her suspiciously. 'I thought you said it was a frog. That looks like a toad to me.'

'Oh,' Courtney said. 'I don't really know the difference.' She looked again at the frog-or-toad. It was larger than she remembered, and browner. 'But anyway, you can tell it's Fraser.'

'Er ... it just looks like a toad to me.'

'But he said "mubbler"!'

Will's brow wrinkled in puzzlement. 'No it didn't!'

'Mubbler,' said the toad.

'There!' Courtney said triumphantly. 'He said it again!'

'No, it didn't!' said Will. 'It said "ribbit"!'

It was Courtney's turn to frown. 'You're hearing things!'

'I'm hearing a toad say "ribbit",' Will pointed out. 'That's what toads say. So I don't think that counts as hearing things.'

'But he didn't say "ribbit"!' Courtney insisted. 'He said "mubbler".'

The toad in her hand went *whooomph*.

Courtney started. 'Did you hear that?'

'I ... heard it go *whooomph*,' Will said cautiously. 'What did you hear?'

'I heard it go *whooomph*, too,' Courtney said. 'But I don't know what that means.'

'Would you two mubblers just shut up?' said the toad. 'This is boring.'

Will went pale.

'There!' Courtney said. 'You heard him speaking that time, didn't you?'

'Er ... no,' said Will. 'I heard it say "woof".'

They stared. 'Is it,' asked Will hesitantly, 'a little bit bigger than before?'

Courtney peered closer. 'His eyes are bulgier, too,' she agreed. 'And he's turned sort of ... reddish?'

Whooomph!

'Er ... it's more kind of grey, now, really,' said Will weakly.

'What are you mubblers on about?' demanded Fraser.

'Well,' said Courtney, 'you just turned into a mouse.'

The mouse sat up and twitched its whiskers. 'Oh, yeah?' it demanded. 'What if I have?'

Without warning, it bit her. Courtney gave a yelp and dropped the mouse on the floor.

'Oi!' it complained. 'What did you do that for?'

'You bit me!' Courtney said, outraged.

'Yeah, well, you deserved it. Accusing me of turning into mice. I never done nothing.'

'I didn't say you did it on purpose!'

'*Courtney Glover*! *William Jackson*!'

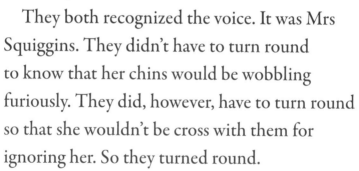

They both recognized the voice. It was Mrs Squiggins. They didn't have to turn round to know that her chins would be wobbling furiously. They did, however, have to turn round so that she wouldn't be cross with them for ignoring her. So they turned round.

'What are you doing, hanging around the corridors?' Mrs Squiggins demanded crossly.

'Er ... we were bringing you this folder,' Will said quickly, holding it out.

Mrs Squiggins looked at the folder accusingly, as though she suspected it might suddenly start talking in assembly. Then she snatched it from Will's hand. 'Well, don't dawdle any more! Back to class!'

'Ah, shut up, Squiggy,' snarled the mouse.

Courtney glanced down warningly.

The mouse blew a raspberry. 'Get lost, mubbler,' it said.

'GO! NOW!' Mrs Squiggins roared.

Having no option, they turned unwillingly towards their classroom. At least, Courtney thought, Mrs Squiggins had not noticed Fraser.

And then she heard a sudden shriek from Mrs Squiggins, a shouted, panicky 'NO!' from the mouse, and the horrific sound of a shoe stamping, hard and deadly, on the corridor floor.

Chapter 6

Without stopping to think, Courtney found herself sprinting back towards Mrs Squiggins, shrieking, 'Fraser!'

Mrs Squiggins froze in mid-stamp and turned her head. 'Fraser?' she enquired coldly.

Courtney sagged in relief as she saw the mouse, still in one piece, cowering in the shadow of Mrs Squiggins' shoe.

'Uh ... yeah ... Fraser,' she panted, rescuing the quivering rodent. 'My ... uh ... my pet mouse.'

'Your pet mouse?' Mrs Squiggins asked disbelievingly. 'Let me see if I understand. You – a child in the same class as Fraser Gribblethwaite – went out and bought a pet mouse, and named it *Fraser*?'

Courtney shrugged. 'Mum wouldn't let me get a rat.'

Mrs Squiggins, chins a-quiver, eyed her suspiciously. 'I'd better not see that mouse again today,' she snarled. 'Or any other day. Because next time, it might not be so lucky.'

'Mubbler,' muttered the mouse, but without any real sense of conviction.

'You won't, Mrs Squiggins,' said Courtney. She stuffed the mouse back into her pocket and she and Will returned to class, where everybody else had just chosen a partner for paired work.

'You two can partner each other,' Mr Barker said understandingly.

'OoooooooOOOOOOOOoooooooh!' went most of the class, and Seema Roy giggled.

OoooooooOOOOOOOOOoooooohs aside, this suited Courtney just fine. She and Will settled down to a fairly easy piece of design work which gave them plenty of time for discussion.

'So now he's a mouse,' Will muttered, bewildered.

'I don't think he *is* a mouse,' Courtney said. 'I just felt him go *whooomph* again.'

'What is he now?'

Courtney shrugged. 'I'm pretty sure he's not a hedgehog,' she said, 'but other than that I've got no idea.'

'How'd it happen?'

'Well … you know how you helped three old women across the road and they gave you some fairy gifts in return? I think this morning they asked Fraser to help them. And … '

Will sighed. 'And he called them mubblers?'

Courtney nodded.

'So they turned him into a frog?' Will asked.

'Well ... I think they all put a spell on him at once. Only, one of them did a frog spell and one did a toad spell, and one did ... '

'A mouse spell?'

'A rat spell, I think. But I reckon the three spells messed each other up so he keeps changing from one kind of animal into another.'

'Or going "woof" when he's a toad,' Will added.

'Anyway, then the old women gave me the gift of understanding animals. Which isn't as useful as you might think, by the way ... '

'But it means you can understand Fraser.'

'Right. But the question is ... what do we do now?'

Will scratched his head. 'I suppose we need to find the old women and get them to change him back.'

Courtney shrugged, doodling idly around the edges of their work. 'How do we do that?'

Will scratched his head harder. 'I think they just turn up. We might see them in school. Last time, they pretended to be dinner ladies.'

Then the bell rang for break time.

Chapter 7

Break time began uneventfully. Apart from the occasional 'OooooooOOOOOOOOooooooh!' from a classmate, Courtney and Will were left mostly to themselves and as soon as she could, Courtney reached into her pocket and pulled out a lizard.

'Mubbler,' said the lizard. 'I don't like your pocket. It's boring.'

Courtney ignored it. 'So,' she said. 'What are we going to do?'

'Well,' said the lizard, 'I'm going for a walk.'

Before Courtney could move, it leapt off her hand and skittered across the playground, narrowly avoiding dozens of running, playing feet.

'No!' Courtney shouted. 'Come back!'

'Ha ha!' taunted the lizard. 'Can't catch me! Can't catch me! Silly old mubbler can't catch me!'

'*Come back*!' Courtney repeated desperately, barging through groups of playing children, Will hot on her heels. 'Fraser! *Fraser*!'

'*Fraser*?' repeated an indignant voice.

Courtney froze.

'I warned you,' said Mrs Squiggins. 'That mouse ... '

'Er ... it's not the mouse this time,' Courtney said feebly, not sure how she was going to explain this.

Mrs Squiggins looked. A number of the children had now noticed Fraser and were pointing and laughing. 'I see,' she said frostily, stalking across the playground as Will and Courtney ran to catch up.

'Can't catch me! You're too slow!' sang Fraser. *Whooomph*! 'Can't catch ... hey!' He waved his legs angrily as Mrs Squiggins lifted him into the air. 'How did the old mubbler move so fast?'

'So,' said Mrs Squiggins, 'you brought your pet mouse to school. And this is yours as well?'

Courtney nodded. 'That's my ... tortoise.'

'Tortoise?' squeaked Fraser, who clearly had not been keeping up with events. 'Tortoise? I thought I was a lizard!'

'So,' Mrs Squiggins said again, 'you have a pet tortoise and a pet mouse – both called Fraser. Are *all* your pets called Fraser?'

Courtney said nothing.

'Well,' said Mrs Squiggins, chins rippling indignantly, 'you won't be seeing *this* one again till the end of the day!'

Mrs Squiggins was wearing a coat with large empty pockets and she slipped Fraser into one of them. Then she turned and marched towards the school building.

She had almost reached it when – with a *whooomph* – Fraser turned into a badger.

Mrs Squiggins' pocket was big enough for a small tortoise. It was not big enough for a small badger, and Fraser was now a large badger. There was a horrendous ripping noise as the pocket tore away from the coat altogether. The badger dropped to the ground and ran.

A badger is an unexpectedly speedy creature when running; but so, it turned out, was Mrs Squiggins. 'Shoo!' she shouted, chasing it madly around the playground. 'Shoo, you brute!'

'Great,' said Courtney heavily. 'We're doomed.'

'Maybe not,' said Will. 'Look who's on playground duty.'

The three old women were making their way across the playground. Courtney ran to meet them.

'You've got to change him back!' she said.

The first old woman shook her head. 'Not until he's learned his lesson.'

Courtney sighed. 'I've been in the same class as Fraser all through school. He's never learned anything!'

'Well, he'd better this time,' said the first old woman.

'Oh, for goodness' sake, Sibyl!' snapped the third. 'Why not change him back now?'

'There is such a thing as tradition, Tracy!' the second one croaked.

'I really think you ought to change him back now,' said Will, whose attention had been drawn by a loud *whooomph* and a lot of screaming.

'Oh, *do* you?' said the first old woman sarcastically. 'And can you give me one good reason why we should?'

'Because,' said Courtney urgently, following Will's gaze, 'if you don't, we'll probably all get trampled by a rhinoceros.'

The old women looked. Sure enough, where the badger had been, there was now a huge, grey rhinoceros. It glared at them all with its little beady eyes ... and charged. Across the playground it thundered, its head lowered as it furiously roared, '**MUBBLERS!**'

'Er ... maybe tradition's not so important after all,' admitted the first old woman.

Hurriedly, the three of them stretched out their hands and, together, muttered something under their breaths.

The rhinoceros charged onwards, filling their vision, and at the last moment, just before it hit them ...

... it turned back into Fraser Gribblethwaite.

'Ow!' said the third old woman, as he bashed into her.

'Mubbler,' Fraser muttered unsteadily. 'I'm going home.'

Without waiting for an answer, he marched across to the entrance gate, pressed the big green button and let himself out.

'He can't just go home!' Will said.

Courtney shrugged. 'He won't get far.'

'How do you know?'

'Well – for one thing, he's wearing his red hoody today. And ... do you see that wolf just across the road ... ?'

The old women were muttering amongst themselves. 'It's not right,' the second was croaking. 'Somebody ought to have learned *something* from all of this. It's tradition. But the mubbler kid hasn't; and I can't see that Courtney or Will has ... '

'Well,' suggested the third, 'perhaps *somebody* might have learned the lesson that they shouldn't go round interfering in other people's lives?'

The other two looked at her in genuine puzzlement. 'No,' said the first after a moment, 'I can't think of anyone who might have learned *that* lesson.'

The third sighed. 'I was afraid you might say that. Come on, let's go.' She turned and began to make her way across the playground. After a couple of steps, she looked back. 'What's keeping you?'

The first two were staring at her in fascination. 'Tracy,' said the first, 'I do believe you're ... hobbling!'

The third old woman gave her a filthy look. 'I'm not *hobbling*,' she said. 'I'm *limping*. That rotten kid was still part-rhinoceros when he stood on my toe.'

'It looks like hobbling to me,' said the second cheerfully. 'I always knew you had it in you!'

'*I'm not hobbling*!' the old woman insisted, making her way painfully towards the gate with the other two merrily hobbling beside her.

Courtney looked around the playground. Most of the children were huddled in groups, in a state of excited shock. Mrs Squiggins, having had a tortoise tear her pocket off by turning into a badger, and having then seen the badger turn into a rhinoceros, had very sensibly fainted and was lying quite peacefully on the tarmac.

'What now?' asked Will.

Courtney heaved a sigh of relief. 'Well,' she said, 'Mrs Squiggins will think she dreamed the whole thing. The kids will all realize there's no point in telling their parents, because they'll just accuse them of making it up. Fraser and the wolf will drive each other mad, and good luck to 'em. *You*,' she continued, slipping her arm through Will's and grinning at him happily, 'can share your chips with me at lunchtime, and then you can be on my team for football. As for those three ... '

She looked over at the three old women, who were hobbling through the gate and turning for home, wherever that was. *Probably*, she thought, *in a land far, far away*.

'As for those three,' she said again, 'they'll all live hobbily ever after.'

About the author

I used to be a teacher, but I escaped when no one was looking and now spend my time hiding in my shed writing stories, or visiting schools to talk about being an author.

The idea for *Twice Upon a Time* came to me when my daughter and I were listening to an audiobook of fairy tales and she pointed out that the fairy's gift in one story might be a little inconvenient in real life.